AutoCAD® 2005

10 Tutorials

1. edition

Frede Uhrskov

Preface

This booklet includes 10 toturials in the use of AutoCAD 2005.

You can use AutoCAD 2005 or 2004. LT users can go through most of the tutorials, but they must notice, that some of the features are not available in LT.

To get the needed files for the toturials, please mail the author at:

frede@uhrskov.com

Place the files in the **Template** directory of your AutoCAD 2005 directory.

Frede Uhrskov

Denmark - spring 2004

Contents

Preface 2

Overview 4

Using the AutoCAD 2005 Tutorial 5

Tutorial 1 - Drawing a Flange 6

Tutorial 2 - Drawing a Room 14

Tutorial 3 - Drawing a Bushing Assembly 21

Tutorial 4 - Drawing a Hub 31

Tutorial 5 - Dimensioning Your Drawing 37

Tutorial 6 - Using Text 45

Tutorial 7 - Drawing a Kitchen Floor Plan 50

Tutorial 8 - Using Attributes 61

Tutorial 9 - Rendering Your Drawing 74

Tutorial 10 - Using Layout and Xrefs 87

Index 93

Overview

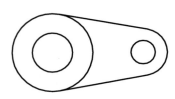

Tutorial 1
Drawing a Flange
Circles, Lines and
object snaps
Fundamental

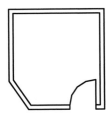

Tutorial 2
Drawing a Room
Multiple parallel lines,
arcs and object snaps
Fundamental

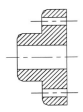

Tutorial 3
Bushing Assembly
Linetypes, layers
and hatching
Fundamental

Tutorial 4
Drawing a Hub
Polyline, 3D
revolved solid.
Fundamental

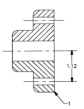

Tutorial 5
Dimensioning
Dimensions
Intermediate

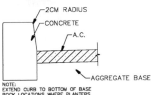

Tutorial 6
Using Text
Text and text styles
Intermediate

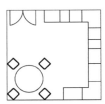

Tutorial 7
Floor Plan
Blocks and arrays
Intermediate

Tutorial 8
Using Attributes
Defining and
editing attributes
Intermediate

Tutorial 9
Rendering
Lights, scenes
and materials.
Advanced

Tutorial 10
Plot preparing
Paper space, model
space and xrefs.
Advanced

Using the AutoCAD 2005 Tutorial

Welcome to the AutoCAD 2005 Tutorial.

You don't have to work through the lessons in the order shown in the overview; however, you should work through lesson 1 first, because it explains how to set up the drawing environment. After lesson 1, gain experience with the other fundamental exercises before moving on to the intermediate exercises. Work through the advanced exercises only when you feel comfortable with the basic commands and functions of AutoCAD.

Entering Commands

Before entering an AutoCAD 2005 command, click the AutoCAD 2005 title bar to make AutoCAD 2005 active.
To cancel any AutoCAD 2005 command, press ESC.
After responding to an AutoCAD 2005 prompt, always press ENTER.
If you make a mistake in your drawing and want to go back and try again, use the UNDO command (enter u ENTER).

Tips

Once you've started AutoCAD 2005, arrange the windows and toolbars so that you have the largest area possible for your drawing.
The exercises may refer to toolbars that are not currently visible. To display the toolbar, choose Toolbars from the View menu, and then choose the toolbar you want to display. If you don't want to display the toolbar or if you can't find it, enter the command on the command line. You can undock toolbars to reveal the name of the specific toolbar.

If the coordinate display doesn't change when you move the cursor, or doesn't display what you expect from the exercise, double-click the Coordinates display on the status bar.

Now you're ready to start the tutorial.

Tutorial 1 - Drawing a Flange

In this first lesson, you will draw a flange. The flange drawing consists of circles, lines, and trimmed areas. You will practice some frequently used AutoCAD 2005 commands: CIRCLE, OFFSET, LINE, MIRROR, and TRIM. Also you will learn some basic AutoCAD 2005 drawing and editing techniques, such as using Object Snap mode.

The lesson consists of six short procedures:

- Creating a new drawing file
- Setting up the drawing environment
- Drawing two bushings
- Drawing a line to connect the bottoms of the bushings using Object Snap mode
- Mirroring the line to connect the tops of the bushings
- Trimming the unwanted lines

To create the drawing file

The file **lesson01** is in the **AutoCAD 2005 Template** directory. For this exercise, you will use the template **lesson01.dwt** upon which to create your drawing. When you are ready to open the template file for this exercise, follow these steps:

1   *From the File menu, choose New.*
2   *In the Create New Drawing dialog box, choose Use a Template.*
3   *In the Select a Template box, select the file **lesson01.dwt** and choose OK.*

AutoCAD 2005 opens a new drawing file using the **lesson01.dwt** template settings. The drawing area should be empty.

To set up the drawing environment

A template drawing contains settings for one or more of the following:

- Drawing units (decimal, engineering, and so on)
- Limits (the boundaries of the drawing)
- Drawing aids (Snap, Grid, Ortho)
- Layers
- Linetypes
- Paper size

In the other Tutorial exercises, the template drawing already has the settings you need. In this first exercise, however, you will learn how to set units, limits, and drawing aids yourself.

1   *From the Format menu, choose Units.*
2   *In the Units dialog box, select 0.00 under Precision and then choose OK.*

AutoCAD 2005 uses decimal units by default, which is the correct setting for this exercise.

What you enter on the command line in response to a prompt is shown in boldface:

Example: Upper right corner <12.0000,9.0000>: **16,12**

3   *From the Format menu, choose Drawing Limits.*
    Reset Model space limits:
    Specify lower left corner or [ON/OFF] <0.0000,0.0000>: *Press ENTER to accept the default*
    Specify upper right corner <12.0000,9.0000>: **16,12**

Note: You must press ENTER after you respond to an AutoCAD 2005 prompt.

You've set the limits of your drawing to 16x12 units, slightly larger than the mechanical part you want to draw. You can see the drawing limits by setting a grid, because a grid extends to the limits.

4   *From the Tools menu, choose Drawing Aids.*
5   *In the Drawing Aids dialog box, select On under Grid.*
6   *Set X spacing under Grid to 0.5 and choose OK. (The Y spacing is automatically set to 0.5 as well.)*

To see the effect of Grid and Limits, you need to zoom the drawing area to the limits of the drawing (ZOOM All). Enter the command on the command line at the bottom of the screen.

> **About the ZOOM Command**
> ZOOM increases or decreases the apparent size of objects. It provides many options for controlling the display of the drawing.

7   *From the Zoom toolbar, choose Zoom All.*

Zoom All looks like this:

The grid now extends to the limits of the drawing.

To draw two bushings

Now that you've set up the drawing environment, you can begin drawing. First draw a circle for the outside of the left bushing.

> **About the CIRCLE Command**
> You can draw a circle in several different ways with the CIRCLE command. In this procedure, you use the center and radius method: you specify the center point, and then specify a radius.

About Absolute Coordinates

In a two-dimensional (2D) coordinate system, you specify points by entering two values that determine the location of a point relative to the X (horizontal) and Y (vertical) axes. The two values are separated by a comma, for example,

0,0
2,3
2.25,6.05

1   *From the Draw toolbar, choose Circle.*

Circle looks like this:

_circle Specify center point for circle or [3P/2P/Ttr (tan tan radius)]: **3,4**
Specify radius of circle or [Diameter]: **2**

Now you will draw another circle for the outside of the right bushing.

2   *From the Draw toolbar, choose Circle.*

AutoCAD 2005 prompts you again to specify the center point using the X and Y axes.

_circle Specify center point for circle or [3P/2P/Ttr (tan tan radius)]: **7.5,4**
Specify radius of circle or [Diameter]: **1.2**

Your drawing should look like this (grid not shown).

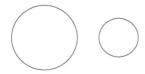

Now you will draw the inside of the left bushing.

3   *From the Modify toolbar, choose Offset.*

Offset looks like this:

About the OFFSET Command

The OFFSET command constructs an object identical to another object, either at a specified distance from the original object or through a specified point, called a through point. In this exercise, you will specify a distance.

Specify the distance on the command line.

Offset distance or [Through] <Through>: **1**

AutoCAD 2005 prompts you to select the object that you want to offset.

Select object to offset or <exit>: *Select the left circle*
The next prompt asks you to indicate the side to which you want to offset the selected object.

Specify point on side to offset: *Select a point anywhere inside the left circle*
Select object to offset or <exit>: *Press ENTER to end OFFSET*

Your drawing should look like this.

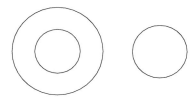

Continue by drawing the inside of the right bushing.

4   *From the Modify toolbar, choose Offset.*

The size of the right bushing is smaller than the left with a radius of 0.6 instead of 1.2.

Offset distance or [Through] <Through>: **0.6**
Select object to offset or <exit>: *Select the right circle*
Specify point on side to offset: *Specify a point anywhere inside the right circle*
Select object to offset or <exit>: *Press ENTER to end OFFSET*

Speed Tip

If you have a two-button mouse, clicking the right mouse button has the same effect as pressing the ENTER key. If you have a pointing device with more buttons, one of them is usually set to ENTER.
In AutoCAD 2005 as well as the LT versions, the right mouse button gives you a shortcut menu, from were you can choose the last command, but that depends on the settings of the **OPTIONS** menu
.

To draw a line to connect the bottoms of the two bushings

You can use the AutoCAD 2005 Object Snap mode to draw lines based on the geometric properties of the objects in your drawing, such as endpoints, midpoints, and center points. In this procedure, you will construct a line tangent to two circles using the Tangent object snap.

1   *From the Draw toolbar, choose Line.*

Line looks like this:

AutoCAD 2005 prompts you to specify the origin of the line you want to draw.

   _line Specify first point:

2   *From the Object Snap toolbar, choose Snap to Tangent.*

Tangent looks like this:

About Selecting with an object snap

When you use any object snap, AutoCAD 2005 adds an additional prompt to indicate what kind of snap is expected. When you specify a point using an object snap, you do not have to specify precisely the point you want; you only need to specify a point that is close enough. You'll notice the yellow circle that jumps to the point indicated by the type of object snap selected.

   _line Specify first point: _tan to: *Select the bottom of the outer-left circle*

AutoCAD 2005 prompts you to specify the other end of the line.

3   *From the Object Snap toolbar, choose Snap to Tangent.*

   Specify next point or [Undo]: _tan to *Select the bottom of the outer-right circle*

AutoCAD 2005 draws the line tangent to the two circles.

   Specify next point or [Undo]: *Press ENTER to end the LINE command*

Your drawing should look like this:

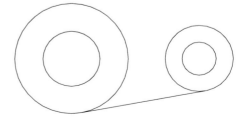

To mirror the line to connect the tops of the bushings

Rather than repeating the LINE command to connect the tops of the bushings, you can use MIRROR. The MIRROR command creates a new copy of an existing object by reflecting it on the other side of an axis defined by two points.

1   *From the Modify toolbar, choose Mirror.*

Mirror looks like this:

The first prompt asks you to select the objects that you want to mirror.

About Object Selection

There are many ways to select objects in AutoCAD. You'll learn several of them in these tutorial exercises. For example, you can select objects by selecting them directly with the pointing device or enclosing them within a window. In this procedure, the quickest selection method is to enter l for "last," because the object you want to mirror was the last object drawn.

_mirror
Select objects: *Enter L to select the last object or pick the wanted object*

AutoCAD 2005 always indicates to you how many objects the selection method found. In this case, it found one.

1 found
Select objects: *Press ENTER to complete object selection*

Next, AutoCAD 2005 prompts you to specify the first point and then the second point of the mirror line. The mirror line is the axis about which AutoCAD 2005 mirrors the selected objects. You will use the Center object snap to draw the mirror line.

Specify first point of mirror line:

2   *From the Object Snap toolbar, choose Snap to Center.*

Snap to Center looks like this:

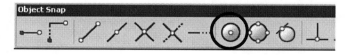

Specify first point of mirror line: _cen of: *Select the outer-left circle*
Specify second point of mirror line: *From the Object Snap toolbar, choose Snap to Center*
Specify first point of mirror line: _cen of
Specify second point of mirror line: _cen of: *Select the right circle*

AutoCAD 2005 asks if you want to delete the old objects (the original line). You want to keep the line, so accept the default of No.

> Delete source objects? [Yes/No] <N>: *Press ENTER to keep the old objects and end the command*

Your drawing should look like this.

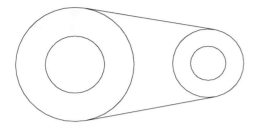

To trim the unwanted portion of the flange

To finish the exercise, you will use the TRIM command to erase part of the circle on the right.

About the TRIM Command

Use the TRIM command to erase objects ending precisely at a cutting edge (or edges) defined by one or more other objects.
When you choose TRIM, AutoCAD 2005 prompts you first to select the objects to use for the cutting edges. AutoCAD 2005 then prompts you to select the objects that you want to trim. The objects are erased up to the cutting edge or edges.

1 From the Modify toolbar, choose Trim.

Trim looks like this:

In this step, you select the lines that are shown in the illustration.

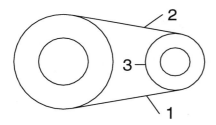

```
_trim
Current settings: Projection=UCS, Edge=None
Select cutting edges ... Select the line (1)
Select objects: Select the line (2)
Select objects: Press ENTER to end the selection of cutting edges
Select object to trim or shift-select to extend or [Project/Edge/Undo]:
Select the circle (3)
Select object to trim or shift-select to extend or [Project/Edge/Undo]:
Press ENTER to end object selection
```

AutoCAD 2005 trims the circle between the two tangent lines.

The finished drawing should look like this:

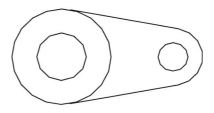

Tutorial 2 - Drawing a Room

In this lesson, you will draw the walls and doorway of a room.
The lesson consists of five short procedures:

- Creating a new drawing file
- Creating a new layer
- Drawing the room walls
- Drawing the door and swing
- Creating a doorway

To create the drawing file

The file **lesson02.dwt** is an AutoCAD 2005 template that contains some of the preliminary setup work for this exercise. To take advantage of this setup, you will create a new file using lesson02.dwt as a template. When you are ready to create the file for this exercise, follow these steps:

1   From the File menu, choose New.
2   In the Create New Drawing dialog box, choose Use a Template.
3   In the Select a Template list box, select the file lesson02.dwt and choose OK.

AutoCAD 2005 opens a new drawing file using the lesson02.dwt template settings. The drawing area should be empty.

To create a new layer

Before you begin drawing the walls, create a new layer called WALLS.

About Layers

Layers are logical groupings of objects in the drawing that work like transparent overlays. You can assign objects to a layer and then control the visibility, color, linetype, and so on.

1   From the Format menu, choose Layer.
2   In the Layer Properties Manager dialog box, choose New, and enter WALLS in the entry field.

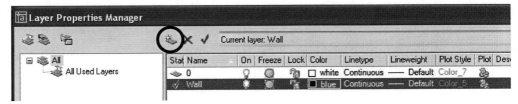

3   Select the color icon in the Color column for the layer WALLS.

4   In the Select Color dialog box, select blue under Index Colors and choose OK.

5   Choose Current and choose OK.

WALLS is now the current layer. Its color is blue.

To draw the room walls

About Relative Coordinates

You can draw lines using absolute coordinates or relative coordinates, which determine the location of a point according to the X and Y axes. Use relative coordinates to draw a series of lines, where each line continues from the endpoint of the previous line. You use the @ sign to tell AutoCAD 2005 that the line starts at the current point.

1   *From the Draw Toolbar, choose Polyline.*

What you enter on the command line in response to a prompt is shown in boldface:

Example: Start point <12.0000,9.0000>: **16,12**

Note: You must press ENTER after you respond to an AutoCAD 2005 prompt.

    _pline
    Specify start point: **36,12**
    Current line-width is 0.00
    Specify next point or [Arc/Close/Halfwidth/Length/Undo/Width]: **@96,0**
    Specify next point or [Arc/Close/Halfwidth/Length/Undo/Width]: **@0,132**
    Specify next point or [Arc/Close/Halfwidth/Length/Undo/Width]: **@-120,0**
    Specify next point or [Arc/Close/Halfwidth/Length/Undo/Width]: **@0,-96**
    Specify next point or [Arc/Close/Halfwidth/Length/Undo/Width]: **c**

1   *From the Modify Toolbar, choose Offset*

Key in the distance: **6**

Click the line

Move the cursor outside the line and click

Your drawing should look like this.

To draw the door and swing

You can begin a line a specific distance in from the wall by using the Tracking metode.

1   *From the Draw toolbar, choose Line.*

Line looks like this:

Place your cursor in the corner - no. 1 - don't click

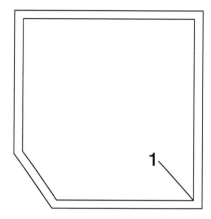

After a little while - move the cursor to the left. You should now be abble to see a thin line along the horizontal line.

Key in **6**

The startpoint of the new line is now placed 6 inches from point number 1

Moved your cursor vertical and

Key in **36**

ENTER

Your drawing should look like this.

Next, make an arc for the door swing.

2   *From the Draw toolbar, choose Arc.*

Arc looks like this: 

In this step, you will specify the points shown in the following illustration.

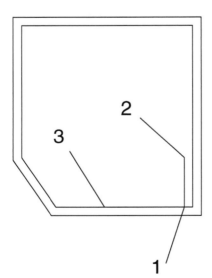

arc Center/<Start point>: **c**
Center: _endp of *Specify the point (1)*
Start point: _endp of *Specify the point (2)*
Angle/Length of chord/<End point>: *From the Object Snap toolbar, choose Snap to Nearest*

Snap to Nearest looks like this:

_nea to *Specify the point (3)*

You've drawn a room with a door.

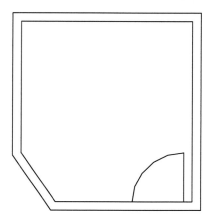

Draw a line from the endpoint of the line and the endpoint of the arc to the opposite line - just like this:

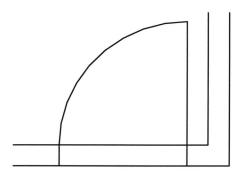

The next step is to create a doorway.

To create a doorway

You use the **TRIM** command to break the wall at the end points of your door and door swing.

1   *From the **Modifytoolbar**, choose Trim*

2   *Pick the 2 small lines that you draw between the 2 polylines - Press ENTER*

3   *Pick the polylines between the 2 small lines - Press ENTER*

Your drawing should now look like this:

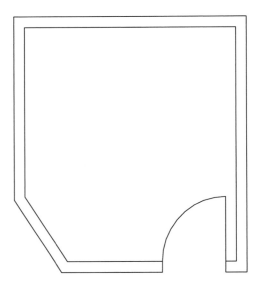

Tutorial 3 - Drawing a Bushing Assembly

In this lesson, you will draw a bushing assembly. The lesson will show you how to draw lines using relative coordinates and will introduce you to layers in AutoCAD. You will also learn about the **FILLET** and **HATCH** commands.

The lesson consists of six short procedures:

- Creating a new drawing file
- Drawing the bottom portion of the bushing assembly
- Changing and modify layers
- Extending center lines of both holes
- Mirroring the bottom portion to the top and fillet the corners
- Hatching the completed outline

To create the drawing file

The file **lesson03.dwt** is an AutoCAD 2005 template that contains some of the preliminary setup work for this exercise. To take advantage of this setup, you will create a new file, using lesson03.dwt as a drawing template. When you are ready to create the file for this exercise, follow these steps:

1   *From the File menu, choose New.*
2   *In the Create New Drawing dialog box, choose Use a Template.*
3   *In the Select a Template list box, select the file lesson03.dwt and choose OK.*

AutoCAD 2005 opens a new drawing file with the lesson03.dwt template settings. The drawing area should be empty.

To draw the bottom part of the bushing assembly

1   *From the Draw toolbar, choose Line.*

Line looks like this:

What you enter on the command line in response to a prompt is shown in boldface:

Note: You must press ENTER after you respond to an AutoCAD 2005 prompt.

       Specify first point: **3,4**
       Specify next point or [Undo]: **@0,-3**
       Specify next point or [Undo]: **@-.75,0**
       Specify next point or [Undo]: **@0,.75**
       Specify next point or [Undo]: **@-.75,0**
       Specify next point or [Undo]: **@0,1.50**

To point: *Press ENTER to end coordinate input*

Your drawing should look like this:

Next, you will change the current layer to **CENTER** before you draw the center lines. The *CENTER* layer has the appropriate linetype and color already assigned to it.

2   *Choose the arrow that is pointing down to the right of the layer display on the Object Properties toolbar.*

AutoCAD 2005 lists the currently defined layers.

3   *Choose CENTER from the list of layers.*

CENTER is now the current layer. Its color is blue.

Continue by drawing the center line of the bottom bolt hole.

4   *From the Draw toolbar, choose Line.*

AutoCAD 2005 prompts you to specify the origin of the line you want to draw. Use the Midpoint Object Snap.

5   *From the Object Snap toolbar, choose Snap to Midpoint.*

Snap to Midpoint looks like this: 

In this step, you will select the lines that are shown in the following illustration.

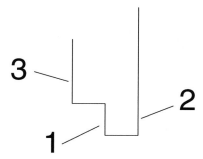

Specify first point:_mid of: *Select the line (1)*

AutoCAD 2005 prompts you to specify the other end of the line you want to draw. Use the Perpendicular Object Snap.

About Perpendicular Object Snap and Ortho Mode:

The drawing file you are working in has been preset to Ortho (Orthogonal) mode. When Ortho mode is on, any lines you draw are constrained to the horizontal and vertical. Perpendicular Object Snap makes sure that the endpoint of the horizontal line lies on the vertical line.

6   *From the Object Snap toolbar, choose Snap to Perpendicular.*

Snap to Perpendicular looks like this:

Specify next point or [Undo]:_per to *Select the line (2)*
Specify next point or [Undo]: *Press ENTER to end the LINE command*

Repeat to draw the center line of the bushing hole.

7   *From the Draw toolbar, choose Line.*

_line Specify first point: *From the Object Snap toolbar, choose Snap to Midpoint*
Specify next point or [Undo]:_mid of: *Select the line (3)*
Specify next point or [Undo]: *From the Object Snap toolbar, choose Snap to Perpendicular*
Specify next point or [Undo]:_per to: *Select the line (2)*
Specify next point or [Undo]: *Press ENTER to end the LINE command*

Now, use the OFFSET command to draw the diameter of the bottom bolt hole.

8   *From the Modify toolbar, choose Offset.*

Offset looks like this:

Specify offset distance or [Through] <Through>: **.125**

In this step, you will select the line that is shown in the following illustration.

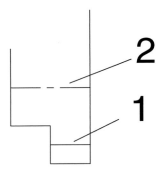

Select object to offset or <exit>: *Select the line (1)*
Specify point on side to offset: *Specify any point below that line*
Select object to offset or <exit>: *Select the line (1) again*
Specify point on side to offset: *Specify any point above that line*
Select object to offset or <exit>: *Press ENTER to end OFFSET*

Repeat to draw the diameter of the bushing hole. Because you'll be mirroring the bottom half of the assembly to create the top half, offset the line for the bottom half only.

9   *Press ENTER to repeat the OFFSET command.*

Specify offset distance or [Through] <Through>: **.375**
Select object to offset or <exit>:: *Select the line (2)*
Specify point on side to offset: *Specify any point below that line*
Select object to offset or <exit>: *Press ENTER to end the command*

Your drawing should look like this:

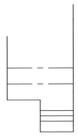

To change layers for the offset lines

Because the lines you just offset are not center lines, you need to change their layers.

1   *Without using any command pick the 3 lines as shown in the picture.*

In this step, you will select the lines that are shown in the following illustration.

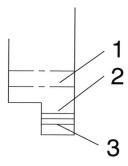

In the drop down list pick the name **edge** to change the layer from **center** to **edge**.

Your drawing should look like this:

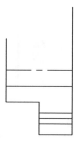

To extend the center lines of both holes

To extend the center lines, you will use the **OFFSET** and **EXTEND** commands.

1   *From the Modify toolbar, choose Offset.*
     Specify offset distance or [Through] <Through>: **.33**

In this step, you will select the lines that are shown in the following illustration.

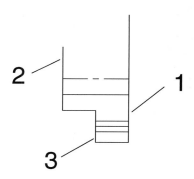

Select object to offset or <exit>: *Select the line (1)*
Side to offset? *Specify any point to the right of that line*
Select object to offset or <exit>: *Select the line (2)*
Specify point on side to offset: *Specify any point to the left of that line*
Select object to offset or <exit>: *Select the line (3)*
Specify point on side to offset: *Specify any point to the left of that line*
Select object to offset or <exit>: *Press ENTER to end the command*

Your drawing should look like this:

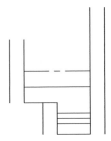

The offset lines you have just drawn are boundary edges. The **EXTEND** command extends the center lines up to those edges.

2   *From the Modify toolbar, choose Extend.*

Extend looks like this:

Select boundary edge(s) (Projmode=UCS, Edgemode=No extend) *Select all three offset lines and press ENTER*
<Select object to extend>/Project/Edge/Undo: *Select near the ends of both blue center lines*
<Select object to extend>/Project/Edge/Undo: *Press ENTER to end the command*

The center lines are extended to meet the offset lines.

The offset lines were temporary construction lines. Now you can erase them.

3   *From the Modify toolbar, choose Erase.*

Erase looks like this:

Select objects: *Select all three offset lines and press ENTER*

Your drawing should look like this:

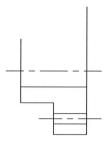

To finish drawing the bushing assembly outline

In this procedure, you will complete the outline of the bushing assembly. First, you will mirror all the objects below the center line of the bushing hole to the top. Then you will fillet (round) the corners of the bushing.

1   *From the Modify toolbar, choose Mirror.*

Mirror looks like this:

The first prompt asks you to select the objects that you want to mirror. Because you need to select several objects at the same time, the quickest way is to draw a selection window around them.
In this step, you specify the points that are shown in the following illustration.

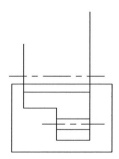

Select objects: *Specify the upper-left corner*
Select objects: Other corner: *Specify the lower-right corner*
Select objects: *Press ENTER to end object selection*

Next, use the Endpoint Object Snap to select the end of the center line.

2   *From the Object Snap toolbar, choose Snap to Endpoint.*

Snap to Endpoint looks like this:

Specify first point of mirror line: _endp of *Specify the left endpoint of the center line*
Specify second point of mirror line: *Specify any point towards the other end of the center line*

Because Ortho mode is on, AutoCAD 2005 mirrors the objects about a perfectly horizontal line.

Delete source objects? [Yes/No] <N>: *Press ENTER to accept the default of No*

Your drawing should look like this:

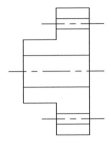

3   *From the Modify toolbar, choose Fillet.*

Fillet looks like this:

Use the FILLET command to round corners to a specific radius. First, set the radius.

Select first object or [Polyline/Radius/Trim/mUltiple]: **r**
Specify fillet radius <0.0000>: **.17**

Your goal is to fillet each corner on the left side of the bushing assembly by selecting pairs of adjacent lines. There are four pairs of lines in all.

4   Select first object or [Polyline/Radius/Trim/mUltiple]: *Select the first of a pair of lines to fillet*
Select first object or [Polyline/Radius/Trim/mUltiple]: *Select the second line to fillet*

5   *Repeat step 4 until you have filleted all four of the exterior corners on the left side.*
Your drawing should look like this:

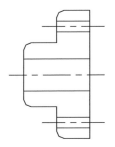

To hatch the completed outline

This procedure shows you how to fill in areas of your drawing with a hatch pattern of diagonal lines. You will choose a hatch pattern and scale it to match your drawing. To begin, change the current layer to **HATCH**.

1   *Choose the arrow that is pointed down to the right of the layer display in the Object Properties toolbar.*

AutoCAD 2005 lists the currently defined layers.

2   *From the list of layers, select HATCH.*

HATCH is displayed. Its color is magenta.
Set the hatch options for pattern and scale.

3   *From the Draw toolbar, choose Hatch.*

Hatch looks like this:

About Hatch Scale

It is usually necessary to scale the hatch pattern to match your drawing. You can easily try out different scales before applying the hatch to the drawing. In this procedure, you enter a value of .75 for the scale.

4   *In the Boundary Hatch dialog box, enter **.75** in the scale field.*

Now you can indicate the areas to hatch by specifying points inside those areas. AutoCAD 2005 determines the boundaries for the hatch automatically.

5   *Choose Pick Points.*

In this step, you will specify the points that are shown in the following illustration:

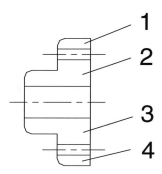

Select internal point: *Specify the point (1)*
Select internal point: *Specify the point (2)*
Select internal point*: Specify the point (3)*
Select internal point: *Specify the point (4)*
Select internal point: *Press ENTER to end selection*

You will normally preview your hatch pattern before you apply it. In this exercise, however, you will omit this step and apply the hatch pattern directly.

6 *In the Boundary Hatch dialog box, choose Apply.*

The finished drawing should look like this:

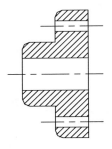

Tutorial 4 - Drawing a Hub

In this lesson, you will make a simple solid model of a wheel hub by drawing a profile in 2D and revolving it to create a 3D model.

The lesson consists of four short procedures:

- Creating the drawing file using a template
- Drawing the profile of the hub with a polyline
- Creating the revolved solid model
- Changing the viewpoint and hiding lines

To create the drawing file

The file **lesson04.dwt** is an AutoCAD 2005 drawing template that contains some of the preliminary setup work for this exercise. To take advantage of this setup, you will create a new drawing file using lesson04.dwt as a template. When you are ready to create the drawing file for this lesson, follow these steps:

1   From the File menu, choose New.
2   In the Create New Drawing dialog box, choose Use a Template.
3   In the Select a Template list box, select the file lesson04.dwt and then choose OK.

AutoCAD 2005 opens a new drawing file based on the lesson04.dwt template file. The drawing area should be empty.

To draw the profile of the hub

A polyline is a series of lines (or lines and arcs) joined together to form one object. In this procedure, you will draw the profile of the hub with a polyline and then revolve it around an axis to create a solid model. You'll use relative polar coordinates to draw a series of polyline segment where each segment continues from the endpoint of the previous segment.

About Polar Coordinates

Polar coordinates specify a distance and an angle in the XY plane, separated by a less than sign (<). Polar coordinates can be either absolute or relative. Because these are relative polar coordinates, you use the at sign (@) at to "tell" AutoCAD 2005 that the line segment starts at the current point.

The illustration shows how AutoCAD 2005 measures angles.

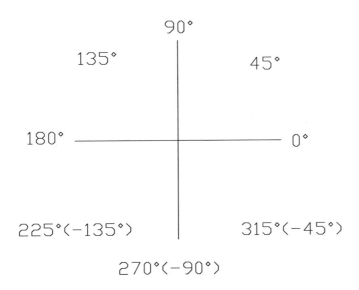

1   *From the Draw toolbar, choose Polyline.*

Polyline looks like this:

What you enter on the command line in response to a prompt is shown in boldface:

Example: Upper right corner <12.0000,9.0000>: **16,12**

Note: You must press ENTER after you respond to an AutoCAD 2005 prompt.

Specify start point: **1,2**
Current line-width is 0.0000
Specify next point or [Arc/Halfwidth/Length/Undo/Width]: **@1<270**

Continue specifying the values and pressing ENTER after each pair of coordinates. If you make a mistake, enter u (Undo) and enter the value again.

Specify next point or [Arc/Close/Halfwidth/Length/Undo/Width]: **@1<0**
Specify next point or [Arc/Close/Halfwidth/Length/Undo/Width]: **@1<270**
Specify next point or [Arc/Close/Halfwidth/Length/Undo/Width]: **@.35<0**
Specify next point or [Arc/Close/Halfwidth/Length/Undo/Width]: **@1.1<90**
Specify next point or [Arc/Close/Halfwidth/Length/Undo/Width]: **@0.1<180**
Specify next point or [Arc/Close/Halfwidth/Length/Undo/Width]: **@0.2<90**
Specify next point or [Arc/Close/Halfwidth/Length/Undo/Width]: **@0.5<180**
Specify next point or [Arc/Close/Halfwidth/Length/Undo/Width]: **@0.7<90**
Specify next point or [Arc/Close/Halfwidth/Length/Undo/Width]: **c**

Your drawing should look like this:

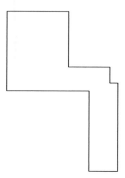

Continue by rounding one of the corners of the section with the FILLET command.

2   *From the Modify toolbar, choose Fillet.*

Fillet looks like this
:

Current settings: Mode = TRIM, Radius = 20.0000
Select first object or [Polyline/Radius/Trim/mUltiple]: **r**
Specify fillet radius <20.0000>: **0.125**
Select first object or [Polyline/Radius/Trim/mUltiple]: *Select the line (1)*
Select second object: *Select the line (2)*

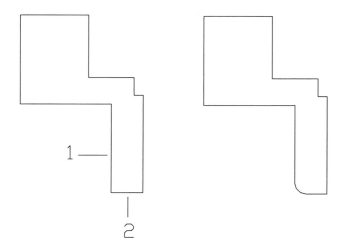

Next, you will chamfer one of the other corners.

About the CHAMFER Command

The CHAMFER command is similar to the FILLET command, only instead of rounding the corner, it cuts off the corner with a straight line. You specify distances from the corner rather than a radius.

4   *From the Modify toolbar, choose Chamfer.*

Chamfer looks like this:

(TRIM mode) Current chamfer Dist1 = 0.0000, Dist2 = 0.0000
Select first line or [Polyline/Distance/Angle/Trim/Method/mUltiple]: **d**
Specify first chamfer distance <15.0000>: **0.125**
Specify second chamfer distance <15.0000>: *Press ENTER to accept the default distance*
Select first line or [Polyline/Distance/Angle/Trim/Method/mUltiple]: *Select the line (1)*
Select second line: *Select the line (2)*

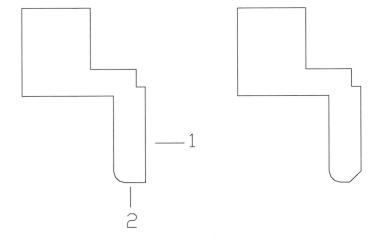

To create a revolved solid model

To create the revolved solid, you will need to specify the polyline and the axis around which it revolves. You can do this by drawing a line specifically for this purpose, or you can specify the start point and endpoint of the axis without drawing a line, as shown in this procedure.

1   *From the View menu, choose Toolbars.*
2   *In the Toolbars list box, choose Solids.*
3   *In the Toolbars dialog box, choose Close.*

AutoCAD 2005 displays the Solids toolbar. Move it to a convenient place on the screen.

4   *From the Solids toolbar, choose Revolve.*

Revolve looks like this:

    Command: _revolve
    Current wire frame density: ISOLINES=4
    Select objects: *Select the polyline*
    Select objects: *Press ENTER to end object selection*
    Specify start point for axis of revolution or define axis by [Object/X (axis)/Y (axis)]:
    1,2.5
    Specify endpoint of axis:Current view direction: VIEWDIR=0.0000,0.0000,1.0000
Specify a view point or [Rotate] <display compass and tripod>: 3,-3,1
  2,2.5

To see that the revolved section really does make a solid, you will specify an angle of revolution of less than 360 degrees. This creates an angled cross section of the model.

    Specify angle of revolution <360>: **225**

AutoCAD 2005 constructs the solid model and displays it in Plan view, as shown in the following illustration.

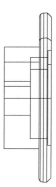

To change the viewpoint and hide lines

This procedure shows you how to view the model in three dimensions and to display it with hidden lines removed so that you can see its structure.

About the VPOINT Command

With VPOINT, you can quickly change the view of a drawing. You specify a viewing position by entering the X, Y, and Z coordinates. In this procedure, the viewpoint is 3 units along the X axis, -3 units down the Y axis, and 1 unit up the Z axis, as shown in the illustration.

1   *On the command line, enter vpoint .*

Current view direction: VIEWDIR=0.0000,0.0000,1.0000
Specify a view point or [Rotate] <display compass and tripod>: **3,-3,1**

Your drawing should look like this:

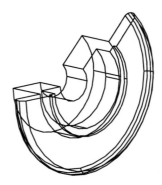

The **HIDE** command displays the model without hidden lines. Now, you can see its solid structure.

2   *From the View menu, choose Toolbars and select the Render toolbar.*

AutoCAD 2005 displays the Render toolbar. Move it to a convenient place on the screen.

3   *In the Toolbars dialog box, choose Close.*
4   *From the Render toolbar, choose Hide.*

Hide looks like this:

AutoCAD 2005 hides the solid model.

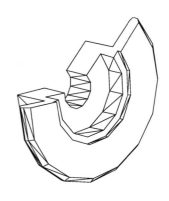

The finished drawing should look like this.

Tutorial 5 - Dimensioning Your Drawing

In this lesson, you will use AutoCAD 2005 commands to add linear-vertical, linear-horizontal, leader, and radial dimensions to your drawing. With AutoCAD 2005 you have full control over how dimensions will appear in your drawing. For example, you can change the arrow size and text size, and save the changes as a new style for future use. In this exercise, you will use the default dimension style.

The lesson consists of five short procedures:

- Creating the drawing file
- Dimensioning the base
- Dimensioning the top edge
- Dimensioning the front
- Dimensioning a radius

To create the drawing file

The file **lesson05.dwt** is an AutoCAD 2005 template which has the object you will dimension in this exercise. To use this template, create a new drawing file, using lesson05.dwt as a template. If you have not already done so, you may want to create a directory for your tutorial exercises, so that you can keep them separate and find them easily. When you are ready to create the drawing file for this exercise, follow these steps:

1   *From the File menu, choose New.*
2   *In the Create New Drawing dialog box, choose Use a Template.*
3   *In the Select a Template list box, select the file lesson05.dwt and choose OK.*

AutoCAD 2005 opens a new drawing file with the lesson05 template settings and existing drawing. The file contains the drawing shown in the following illustration.

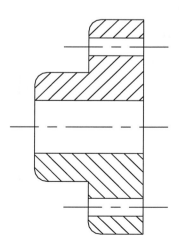

To dimension the base

What you enter on the command line in response to a prompt is shown in boldface:

Example: Upper right corner <12.0000,9.0000>: **16,12**

Note: You must press ENTER after you respond to an AutoCAD 2005 prompt.
Remember that you must press ENTER whenever you enter a response to an AutoCAD 2005 prompt.

1   *From the View menu, choose Toolbars and then choose Dimension.*

AutoCAD 2005 displays the Dimension toolbar. Move it to a convenient place on the screen.

2   *In the Toolbars dialog box, select Close.*

Setting a running object snap makes it easier to snap to the intersections of lines.

3   *From the Tools menu, choose Object Snap Settings.*
4   *In the Osnap Settings dialog box, on the Running Osnap tab, select the Intersection checkbox and choose OK.*
5   *From the Dimension toolbar, choose Linear Dimension.*

Linear Dimension looks like this:

In this step, you will specify the points that are shown in the following illustration.

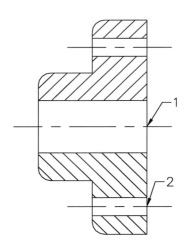

Specify first extension line origin or <select object>: *Specify the point (1)*
Specify second extension line origin: *Specify the point (2)*

AutoCAD 2005 will prompt you for the location of the dimension. Any point will do, as long as it provides enough room for the dimension text. A distance of 3.6 on the X axis is a good approximation. You can check the location by reading the coordinate display in the AutoCAD 2005 status bar at the bottom of the drawing screen.

> Specify dimension line location or [Mtext/Text/Angle/Horizontal/Vertical/Rotated]:
> *Specify a point at about 3.6 on the X-axis*

Your drawing should look like this:

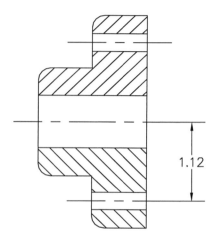

About the Continue Option

Starting at the center of the base and working downward ensures that the second dimension does not overlay the first as you continued dimensioning with the Continue option. By using this option, you can start the next dimension at the endpoint of the last dimension, rather than specifying both first and second origin points.

6   *From the Dimension toolbar, choose Continued Dimension.*

Continued Dimension looks like this:

In this step, you will specify the point that is shown in the following illustration.

> Specify a second extension line origin or [Undo/Select] <Select>: *Specify the point (1)*
> Specify a second extension line origin or [Undo/Select] <Select>: *Press ENTER*
> Select continued dimension: *Press ENTER*

To dimension the top edge

Dimension the top edge with the same method from the previous procedure, by drawing the first dimension and then continuing directly with the second. The endpoints that you measure from in this procedure are the endpoints of arcs created by the FILLET command. Set the running object snap to snap to the endpoints of lines.

1   *From the Tools menu, select Object Snap Settings.*
2   *In the Osnap settings dialog box, on the Running Osnap tab, choose Endpoint.*
3   *In the Osnap settings dialog box, choose OK.*
4   *From the Dimension toolbar, choose Linear Dimension.*

In this step, you will specify the points that are shown in the following illustration.

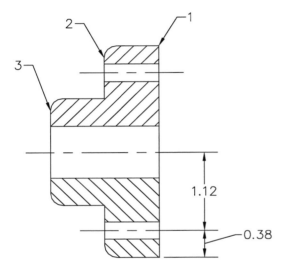

Specify first extension line origin or <select object>: *Specify the point (1)*
Specify second extension line origin: *Specify the point (2)*
Specify dimension line location or [Mtext/Text/Angle/Horizontal/Vertical/Rotated]: *Select a point at about 3.00,4.50*

5   *From the Dimension toolbar, choose Baseline Dimension.*

Baseline Dimension looks like this:

Specify a second extension line origin or [Undo/Select] <Select>: *Specify the point (3)*
Specify a second extension line origin or [Undo/Select] <Select>: *Press ENTER*

Your drawing should look like this:

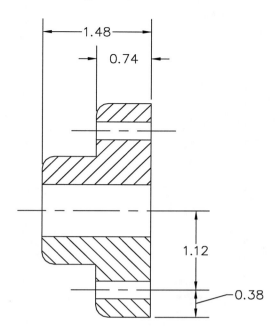

To dimension the front

Repeat the previous sequence to dimension the front.

1   *From the Dimension toolbar,*
     choose Linear Dimension.

In this step, you will specify the points that
are shown in the following illustration.

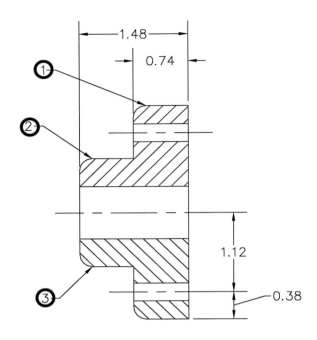

Specify first extension line origin or <select object>: *Specify the point (1)*
Specify second extension line origin: *Specify the point (2)*
Specify dimension line location or [Mtext/Text/Angle/Horizontal/Vertical/Rotated]: *Select*
a point at about 0.45,3.60

2   *From the Dimensioning toolbar, choose Continued Dimension.*
     Specify a second extension line origin or [Undo/Select] <Select>: *Specify the point (3)*
     Specify a second extension line origin or [Undo/Select] <Select>: *Press ENTER*
     Specify a second extension line origin or [Undo/Select] <Select>: *Press ENTER*

Your drawing should look like this:

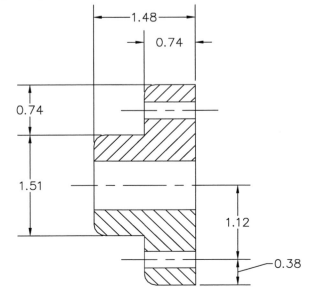

3   *From the Dimension toolbar, choose Linear Dimension.*
In this step, you will specify the points that are shown in the following illustration.

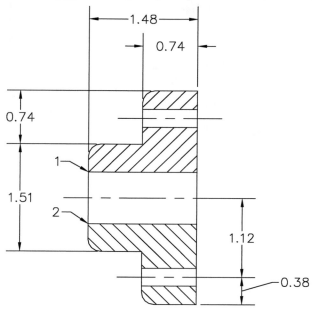

Specify first extension line origin or <select object>: *Specify the point (1)*
Specify second extension line origin: *Specify the point (2)*
Specify dimension line location or [Mtext/Text/Angle/Horizontal/Vertical/Rotated]:
Select a point at about 1.00,2.50

Your drawing should look like this.

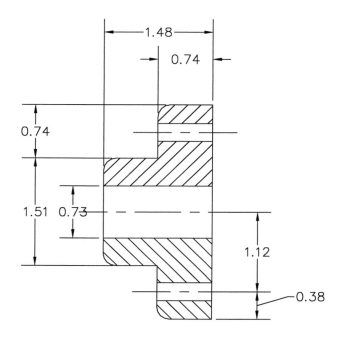

To dimension a radius

To finish the exercise, you will add a dimension showing the radius of the corner fillet.

1   *From the Dimension toolbar, choose Radius Dimension.*

Radius dimension looks like this:

In this step, you will specify the point that is shown in the following illustration.

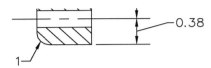

Select arc or circle: *Select the arc (1)*
Specify dimension line location or [Mtext/Text/Angle]: *Drag the leader line to the correct location and click*

The finished drawing should look like this.

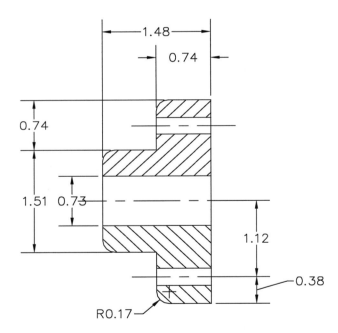

Tutorial 6 - Using Text

This lesson demonstrates how to set text styles and place text in a drawing. To place text, you can use paragraph text, that is, text that contains multiple lines and formatting, or you can use line text, which consists of single lines.

The lesson consists of five short procedures:

- Creating the drawing file from a template.
- Creating a new text style
- Creating paragraph text
- Drawing leaders with text
- Writing a single line of text

To create the drawing file

The file **lesson06.dwt** is an AutoCAD 2005 drawing that contains some of the preliminary setup work for this exercise. To take advantage of this setup, you will create a new file, using lesson06.dwt as a template. If you have not already done so, you may want to create a directory for your tutorial exercises, so that you can keep them separate and find them easily. When you are ready to create the file for this exercise, follow these steps:

1   *From the File menu, choose New.*
2   *In the Create New Drawing dialog box, choose Use a Template.*
3   *In the Select a Template list box, select the file lesson06.dwt and choose OK.*

AutoCAD 2005 opens a new drawing file using the settings from the template you specified. The drawing area contains the drawing shown in the following illustration.

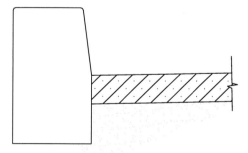

To create a new text style

First, add text in the default text style.
Note: You must press ENTER after you respond to an AutoCAD 2005 prompt.

About Text Height

After you name the text style, you select the font file to use as a prototype for the new style. You can then modify the font, for example, by changing its height. If you leave the height set to 0, AutoCAD 2005 prompts you for the height each time you use the text style. This is useful when you want to use the same text style with different heights in the same drawing.

1   *From the Format menu, choose Text Style.*
2   *In the Text Style dialog box, under Style Name, choose New.*
3   *In the New Text Style dialog box, under Style Name, type NOTES and choose OK.*
4   *Under Font Name in the Text Style dialog box, select simplex.shx, and under height, enter 0.00.*
5   *In the Text Style dialog box, choose Apply, and then choose Close.*

The current text style is now NOTES.

To create paragraph text

You will use the Multiline Text Editor to format and enter paragraph text. Before creating the text, you will define a rectangular text boundary that controls the width of the paragraph.

1   *From the Draw toolbar, choose Multiline Text.*

Multiline Text looks like this:

Specify First Corner: **-2,0**
Specify opposite corner or [Height/Justify/Rotation/Style/Width]: **5,-5**

2   *In the Multiline Text Editor dialog box, enter the following text.*

After NOTE: press ENTER but allow the other text to wrap from one line to the next. Do not choose OK before you have completed steps 3 and 4.

NOTE:
EXTEND CURB TO BOTTOM OF BASE ROCK AT LOCATIONS WHERE PLANTERS MEET PAVEMENT. CHECK CITY CODE.

3   *In the Multiline Text Editor dialog box, highlight the text NOTE: and in the Charactertab, choose the Text Color list box.*
4   *In the Select Color list box, select Magenta.*
5   *In the Multiline Text Editor dialog box, choose OK.*

The drawing should look like this.

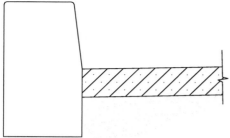

NOTE:
EXTEND CURB TO BOTTOM OF BASE
ROCK LOCATIONS WHERE PLANTERS
MEET PAVEMENT. CHECK CITY CODE.

To draw leaders with attached notes

You can use the LEADER command to draw leaders with notes formatted as line or paragraph text. In this procedure, you will draw four leaders, each with a single line of text.

In this step, you will specify the points that are shown in the illustration.

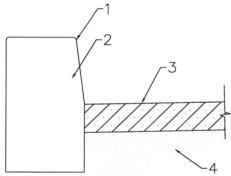

NOTE:
EXTEND CURB TO BOTTOM OF BASE
ROCK LOCATIONS WHERE PLANTERS
MEET PAVEMENT. CHECK CITY CODE.

1   *From the Dimension toolbar, choose QuickLeader.*

Specify first leader point, or [Settings] <Settings>: *Specify a point (1)*
Specify next point: *Specify a point diagonally up and to the right*
Specify next point: *Press ENTER*
Specify text width <0.00>: *Press ENTER*
Enter first line of annotation text <Mtext>: **2CM RADIUS**
Enter next line of annotation text: *Press ENTER*

Repeat the LEADER command to draw the other leaders with their text.

2   *Press ENTER to repeat the LEADER command.*

Specify first leader point, or [Settings] <Settings>: *Specify a point (2)*
Specify next point: *Specify a point diagonally up and to the right*
Specify next point: *Press ENTER*
Enter first line of annotation text <Mtext>: **CONCRETE**
Enter next line of annotation text: *Press ENTER*

3   *Press ENTER to repeat the LEADER command.*

Specify first leader point, or [Settings] <Settings>: *Specify a point (3)*
Specify next point: *Specify a point diagonally up and to the right*
Specify next point: *Press ENTER*
Enter first line of annotation text <Mtext>: **A.C.**
Enter next line of annotation text: *Press ENTER*

4   Press ENTER to repeat the LEADER command.

Specify first leader point, or [Settings] <Settings>: *Specify a point (4)*
Specify next point: *Specify a point diagonally down and to the right*
Specify next point: *Press ENTER*
Enter first line of annotation text <Mtext>: **AGGREGATE BASE**
Enter next line of annotation text: *Press ENTER*

Your drawing should look like this.

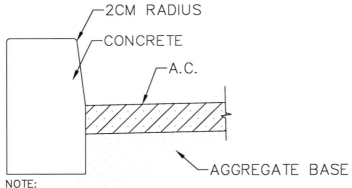

NOTE:
EXTEND CURB TO BOTTOM OF BASE
ROCK LOCATIONS WHERE PLANTERS
MEET PAVEMENT. CHECK CITY CODE.

To create a single line of text

For a single line of text that does not require formatting, you will use the DTEXT (Dynamic Text) command. DTEXT uses the named style NOTES that you have created earlier. AutoCAD 2005 will prompt you to enter the height of the text because you did not specify a height for the style.

1   *From the Text Toolbar choose Dtext.*

   Current text style: "ROMANC" Text height: 0.05
   Specify start point of text or [Justify/Style]: **-0.5,-3**
   Specify height <0.05>: **0.4**
   Specify rotation angle of text <0>: *Press ENTER*
   Enter text: *CURB DETAIL*
   Enter text: *Press ENTER*

The finished drawing should look like this.

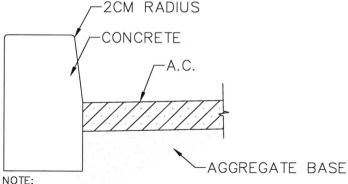

Tutorial 7 - Drawing a Kitchen Floor Plan

In this lesson, you will use AutoCAD 2005 commands to draw a kitchen.
The lesson consists of five short procedures:

- Creating a new drawing file
- Drawing the kitchen doors
- Drawing a chair
- Making the chair into a block
- Drawing a table and insert the chairs

To create the drawing file

The file **lesson07.dwt** is an AutoCAD 2005 template that contains some of the preliminary
setup work for this exercise. To take advantage of this setup, you will create a new file using
lesson07.dwt as a template. When you are ready to create the file for this exercise, follow these
steps:

1   *From the File menu, choose New.*
2   *In the Create New Drawing dialog box, choose Use a Template.*
3   *In the Select a Template box, select the file lesson07.dwt and choose OK.*

AutoCAD 2005 opens a new drawing file with settings from the **lesson07.dwt** template. The
drawing area should contain the drawing shown in the illustration. The drawing shows a kitchen
floor plan with standard-size cabinets drawn with the **LINE**, **OFFSET**, and **TRIM** commands.

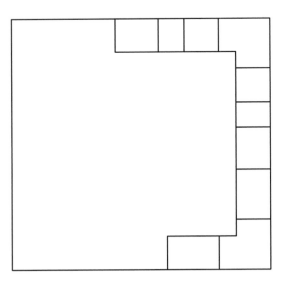

To draw the kitchen doors

What you enter on the command line in response to a prompt is shown in boldface:

EXAMPLE: Upper right corner <12.0000,9.0000>: **16,12**

Note: You must press ENTER after you respond to an AutoCAD 2005 prompt.

1   *From the Draw toolbar, choose Line.*

Line looks like this:

In this step, you will specify the points that are shown in the following illustration.

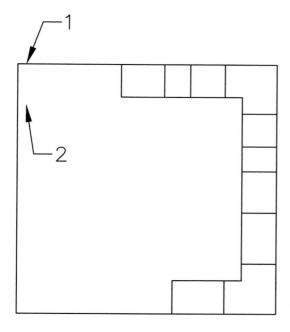

> _line Specify first point: *Specify the point (1) at coordinates 12,186*
> Specify next point or [Undo]: *Specify the point (2) at coordinates 12,156*
> Specify next point or [Undo]: *Press ENTER to end Line input*

Now you need an arc for the door swing. There are many ways to draw an arc in AutoCAD 2005. In this procedure, you will use the **Start Point, Center, End Point** method.

2   From the Draw toolbar, choose Arc.

Arc looks like this:

In this step, you will specify the points that are shown in the following illustration.

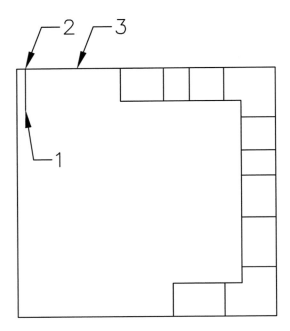

Command: _arc Specify start point of arc or [Center]: *Specify the start point (1)*
Specify second point of arc or [Center/End]: **c**
Specify center point of arc: *Specify the center point (2)*
Specify end point of arc or [Angle/chord Length]: *Specify the end point (3)*

Your drawing should now look like this:

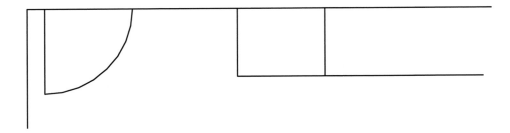

You add the second door by using the **MIRROR** command.

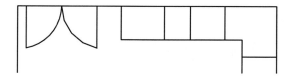

3   *From the Modify toolbar, choose Mirror.*

Mirror looks like this:

Specify the lines and points that are shown in the following illustration.

Select objects: *Select the line (1) and the arc (2)*
Select objects: *Press ENTER to end object selection*
Specify first point of mirror line: *Specify the point (3)*
 Specify second point of mirror line: *Specify any point (4) directly below point (3) -
Ortho on*
Delete source objects? [Yes/No] <N>: *Press ENTER*

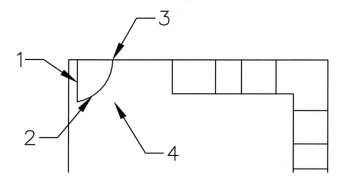

Your drawing should now look like this:

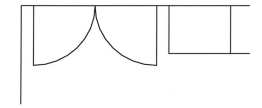

To draw a chair

1   *From the Draw toolbar, choose Polygon.*

Polygon looks like this:

In this step, you will specify the point that are shown in the following illustration:

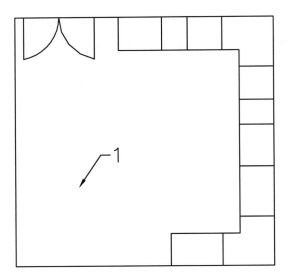

_polygon Enter number of sides <4>: *Press ENTER to accept the default value of 4*
Specify center of polygon or [Edge]: *Specify any point 1 near the lower left of the drawing*
Enter an option [Inscribed in circle/Circumscribed about circle] <I>: *Press ENTER*
Specify radius of circle: **12**

2   *On the status bar, click Snap to turn off Snap mode.*
3   *From the Modify toolbar, choose Offset.*

Offset looks like this:

Specify offset distance or [Through] <Through>: **1**
Select object to offset or <exit>: *Select the square*
Specify point on side to offset: *Specify a point inside the square*
Select object to offset or <exit>: *Press ENTER to end OFFSET input*

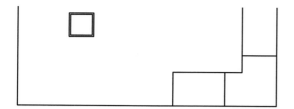

You will use the **FILLET** command to round the corners of the chair. First you will zoom in on the chair by drawing a window around it.

4   *From the Standard toolbar, choose Zoom Window.*

   Zoom Window looks like this:

   Specify first corner: *Specify a point above and to the left of the chair*
   Specify opposite corner: *Specify a point below and to the right of the chair*

5   *From the Modify toolbar, choose Fillet.*

   Fillet looks like this:

   Current settings: Mode = TRIM, Radius = 2.00
   Select first object or [Polyline/Radius/Trim/mUltiple]: **r**
   Specify fillet radius <2.00>: **2**

6   Fillet the first corner

In this step, you select the lines shown in the following illustration.

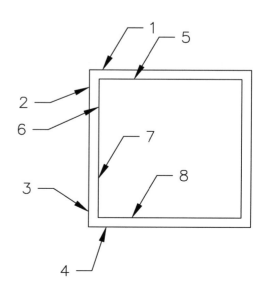

Command: *Press ENTER to restart the FILLET command*
Select first object or [Polyline/Radius/Trim/mUltiple]: *Select the line (1)*
Select second object: *Select the line (2)*

7   *Repeat step 6 to fillet the other pairs of lines: 3 and 4, 5 and 6, 7, and 8.*

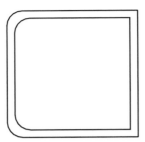

8   *From the Standard toolbar, choose Zoom Previous.*

Zoom Previous looks like this:

Blocks save you time by allowing you to reuse parts of your drawing and reduce file size. The following two procedures will demonstrate how to work with blocks.

First, you'll make the chair that you just drew into a block, and then you will draw a table. Later, instead of drawing each chair individually, you will insert that block and copy it for each instance of a chair.

To make the chair into a block

1   *On the command line, enter block.*

      In the dialogbox name the block as **CHAIR**

The point you select for the insertion base point becomes the insertion point for the **CHAIR** block. You will use the midpoint of the left side of the chair.

      Choose **Pick point as shown**

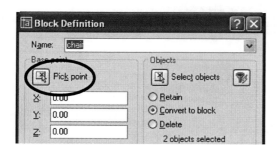

2   *From the Object Snap toolbar, choose Snap to Midpoint.*

Snap to Midpoint looks like this:

In this step, you will select the line that is shown in the following illustration.

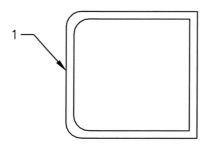

BLOCK Specify insertion base point:_*mid of Select the line (1)*
Select objects: *Draw a window around the chair as you did for ZOOM*
Select objects: *Press ENTER to end object selection*

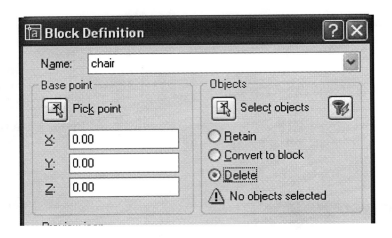

*Mark the **Delete** radio button*
Choose OK

Although the chair is not displayed in the drawing, it's been stored as a block in your drawing database. You'll insert it in a moment.

To draw the table and insert the chairs

1   *At the status bar, click Snap to turn on Snap mode.*
2   *From the Draw toolbar, choose Circle*

Circle looks like this:

Specify center point for circle or [3P/2P/Ttr (tan tan radius)]: *Specify a point at coordinates 48,48*
Radius: **27**

3   *On the command line, enter insert .*

The **INSERT** command opens the insert dialogboks, where you can choose the block named **CHAIR**

Make the dialogbox look like the picture below:

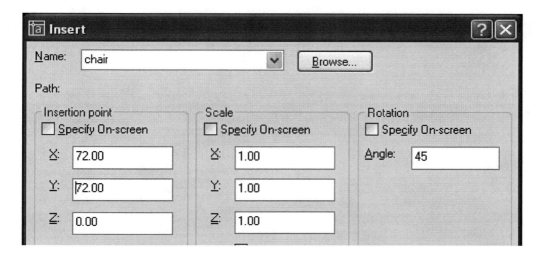

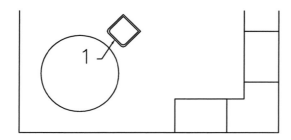

*Click **OK***

The chair is inserted in the drawing at an angle of 45 degrees.

You will now use the ARRAY command to make three copies of the chair and place them in position around the table.

4 *From the Modify toolbar, choose Array.*

Array looks like this:

*Get the array dialogbox look like this - click the **Select Objects** button and choose the chair.*

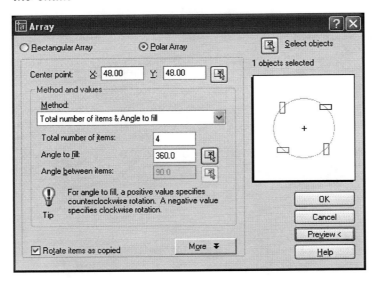

*Click **OK***

The finished drawing should look like this.

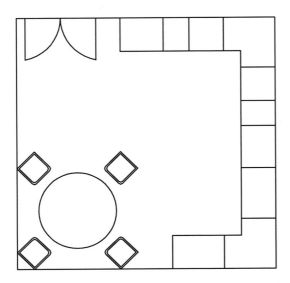

Tutorial 8 - Using Attributes

This lesson demonstrates some of the ways you can use AutoCAD 2005 to manage facilities. The lesson focuses on managing the nongraphic data associated with objects in an AutoCAD 2005 drawing: for example, the model and cost data assigned to tables, chairs, and telephones in an office.

The lesson consists of seven short procedures:

- Creating a new drawing file
- Adding a table and define attributes for it
- Making the table into a block and insert it in the drawing
- Erasing objects from the office layout
- Moving the computer
- Editing the attributes
- Calculating the area of a cubicle

To create the drawing file

The file **lesson08.dwt** is an AutoCAD 2005 template that contains some of the preliminary setup work for this exercise. To take advantage of this setup, you will create a new drawing file using **lesson08.dwt** as a template. When you are ready to create the file for this exercise, follow these steps:

1   *From the File menu, choose New.*
2   *In the Create New Drawing dialog box, choose Use a Template.*
3   *In the Select a Template list box, select the template lesson08.dwt and choose OK.*

AutoCAD 2005 opens a new drawing file with the settings from the template you specified. It contains the floor plan shown in the illustration.

The drawing is in this illustration rotated 90 degrees.

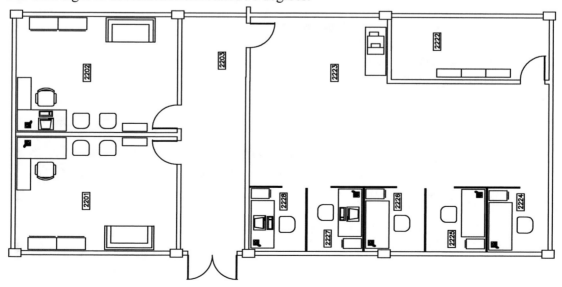

In this procedure, you will draw a table and then assign manufacturer, cost, purchase date, and other information to it. You will do this by defining a series of attributes. An attribute is a label, or tag, that is attached to a particular block and stored along with it.

What you enter on the command line in response to a prompt is shown in boldface:

EXAMPLE: Upper right corner <12.0000,9.0000>: **16,12**

Note: You must press ENTER after you respond to an AutoCAD 2005 prompt.

To add a table and define attributes for it

1   *From the standard toolbar, choose Zoom Window.*

Zoom Window looks like this:

In this step, you will specify the points that are shown in the following illustration.

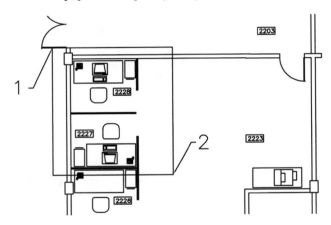

Specify first corner: *Specify the point (1)*
Specify opposite corner: *Specify the point (2)*

AutoCAD 2005 zooms in on the window you selected so that it fills the screen. Next you will draw a rectangle for the table.

2   *From the Draw toolbar, choose Rectangle.*

Rectangle looks like this:

By reading the coordinates display in the status bar, you can see which points to specify.

In this step, you will specify the points that are shown in the following illustration.

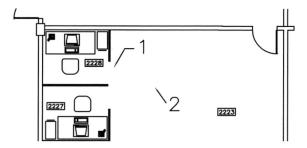

> Specify first corner point or [Chamfer/Elevation/Fillet/Thickness/Width]: *Specify the point (1) at coordinates 114,390*
> Specify other corner point or [Dimensions]: *Specify the point (2) at coordinates 174,360*

You will use a dialog box to define attributes for the table.

3 *On the command line, enter att*

Make the dialogbox look like this:

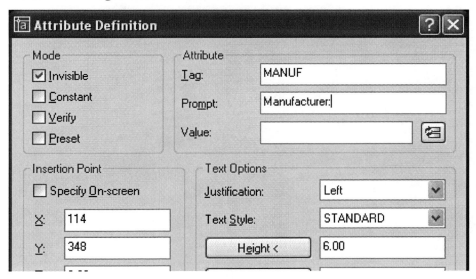

The tag is the label for the attribute. The prompt is the message that's displayed when you insert the block. In this case, the prompt requests the manufacturer's name.

4   *Choose OK.*

AutoCAD 2005 displays the attribute below the table at the insertion point you specified.

Your drawing should look like this:

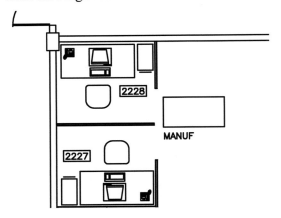

5   *Press ENTER to repeat the command.*

   Enter the following information for the Tag and Prompt values.

Note: Select the Align Below Previous attribute. (This saves you from selecting the insertion point each time.)

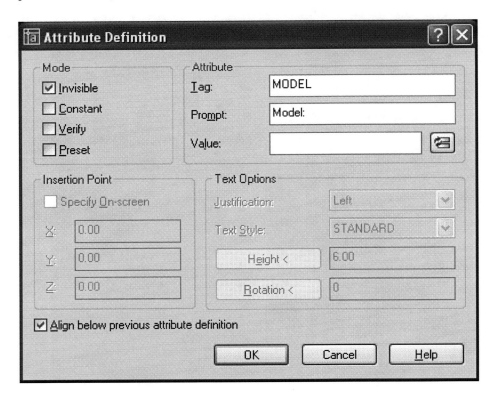

Choose OK. Repeat this process to add these last two strings.

Tag   Prompt

COST   **Cost:**
LOCATION   **Location:**

Your drawing should look like this.

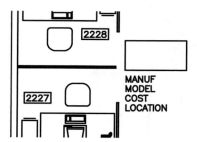

Now, you'll make the table and attributes into a block that you can insert easily in other places in the drawing.

To make the table into a block and insert it in the drawing

1   *On the command line, enter block.*

Enter the information shown in the dialogbox:

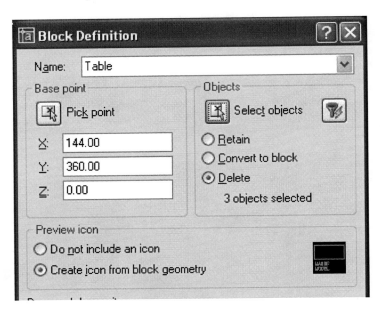

Although the table is not displayed in the drawing, it is stored as a block in your drawing database. You'll insert it in the drawing now.

2   *On the command line, enter insert.*

Enter the information shown in the dialogbox:

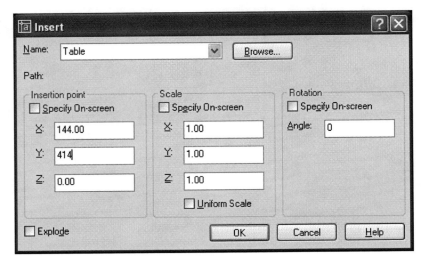

Choose OK

You are prompted to enter actual values for the attributes. The Enter Attributes dialog box displays the prompts you defined earlier.

3   *Respond by entering the following values:*

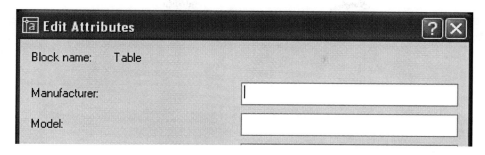

Note: The prompts may not appear in exactly the order shown.

     Location: **2227**
     Model: **Tressle**
     Manufacturer: **Sierra Furniture**
     Cost: **126.00**

4   *Choose OK.*

The table is inserted with all the information defined for it. You can't see the attributes at this point because you made them invisible. Attributes can be made visible using the **ATTDISP** command.

The next procedures will demonstrate how to modify information in an AutoCAD 2005 drawing. Suppose that employee Terri in cubicle 2228 has been promoted and is scheduled to move into office 2201. You want to record the following changes in the office drawing:
Terri takes her computer to 2201 but leaves the office furniture.
Cubicles 2228 and 2227 are combined to create one large cubicle, 2227.
Dean, the current occupant of 2227, keeps his computer and furniture and acquires the furniture in 2228.

To erase objects from the office layout

Use the Zoom Window in the drawing so you have a better view of the area in which you want to work. See the broken line below:

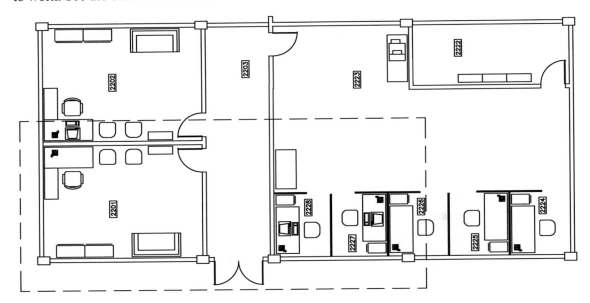

You will erase the objects that are no longer needed in the drawing.

1   *From the Modify toolbar, choose Erase.*

Erase looks like this:

Select the objects shown in the following illustration. Do not erase item #6 (the computer). You will use it later in this exercise.

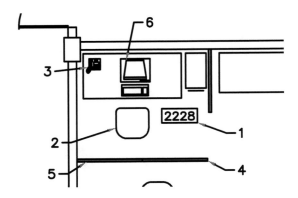

Select objects: *Select the room tag (1)*
Select objects: *Select the chair (2)*
Select objects: *Select the telephone (3)*
Select objects: *Select the two parts of the partition (4, 5)*
Select objects: *Press ENTER to end the command*

Now, move Terri's computer to its new location.

To move the computer

1   *From the Modify toolbar, choose Rotate.*

Rotate looks like this:

Select objects: *Select the computer (6)*
Select objects: *Press ENTER to end selection*
Specify base point: *From the Object Snap toolbar, choose Snap to Intersection*

Snap to Intersection looks like this:

int of: *Select the lower-left corner of the computer*
Specify rotation angle or [Reference]: **270**

2   *From the Modify toolbar, choose Move.*

Move looks like this:

In this step, you will specify the points that are shown in the following illustration.

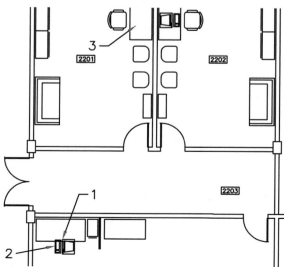

Select objects: *Select the computer (1)*
Select objects: *Press ENTER to end selection*
Specify base point or displacement: *From the Object Snap toolbar, choose Snap to Midpoint*
_MID of *Select the base of the computer (2)*
Specify second point of displacement or <use first point as displacement>: *Specify the point (3)*

Next, you will change the attributes for the room tag, telephone, and computer in room 2201.

To edit the attributes

In this step, you will select the objects that are shown in the following illustration.

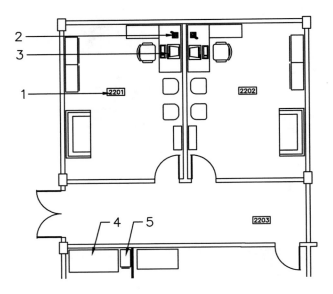

1	*On the command line, enter ddatte .*
	Select block: *Select the room tag (1)*
2	*In the Edit Attributes dialog box, enter the name* **Terri Napier** *for Employee.*
3	*Choose OK.*
4	*Press ENTER to repeat the* **DDATTE** *command.*
	Select block: *Select the telephone (2)*
5	*Enter* **Terri Napier** *for Employee and choose OK.*
6	*Press ENTER to repeat the* **DDATTE** *command.*
	Select block: *Select the computer (3)*
7	*Change the location to* **2201** *and choose OK.*
8	*Repeat the procedure for the desk (4) and file cabinet (5) in Terri's old cubicle, 2228, changing the location to* **2227***.*

The cubicle has doubled in size, so you may want to calculate the new area. You can do this easily with AutoCAD.

To calculate the area of the cubicle

1   *Zoom in on the 2227 cubicle area using ZOOM.*

2   *Choose the polyline command*

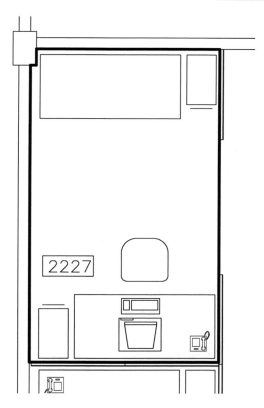

Draw a polyline as shown - the thick line

3   *Choose multilinetext*

Draw a textbox in the empty area of the cibicle and write the text Area =

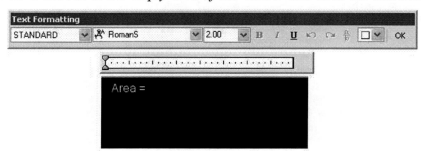

4   *Right click in the text area and choose* **Insert Field...**

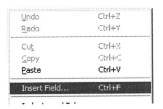

Choose **All** *inthe* **Field category** *and* **Object** *in   the* **Field names**

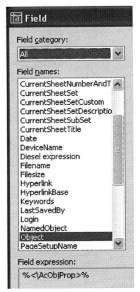

,

5   *Select the Select object button*

Pick the polyline and press ENTER

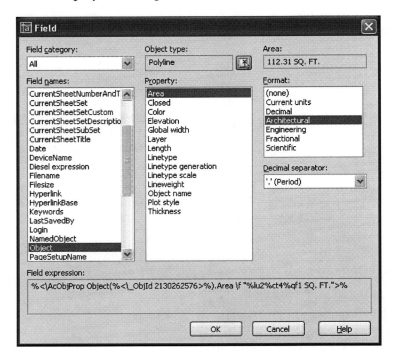

AutoCAD 2005 displays the result.

6   *Click OK*

Now the result is shown in the textbox in AutoCAD. The area result is shown with a light grey background. The background color is a visual cue that this part of the text is a field.

Tutorial 9 - Rendering Your Drawing

Rendering is the application of color, light, and shading to a drawing. This exercise shows you some of AutoCAD's rendering capabilities. Before you begin, make sure your hardware can display 16 mill. colors and Windows is set up to display 16 mill. colors. If your hardware only displays 256 colors, you can't use RENDER effectively. The screen resolution setting must be 800x600 or higher. For more information about configuring for RENDER, see the AutoCAD 2005 Installation Guide. In AutoCAD 2005 you can render with true color in 24 bit.

Note This lesson has no demo.
The lesson consists of 10 short procedures:

- Creating the drawing file
- Seeing the effect of smooth shading
- Saving named views
- Adding lights
- Creating scenes
- Rendering using scenes
- Creating new materials
- Attaching materials to colors
- Rendering the final image

To create the drawing file

The file **lesson09.dwt** is an AutoCAD 2005 template that contains some of the preliminary setup work for this exercise. To take advantage of this setup, you will create a new drawing file using **lesson09.dwt** as a template. When you are ready to create the file for this exercise, follow these steps:

1   *From the File menu, choose New.*
2   *In the Create New Drawing dialog box, choose Use a Template.*
3   *In the Select a Template list box, select the file lesson09.dwt and choose OK.*

AutoCAD 2005 opens a new drawing file using the settings from the template you specified. The drawing area contains four views of a microscope, as shown in the following illustration.

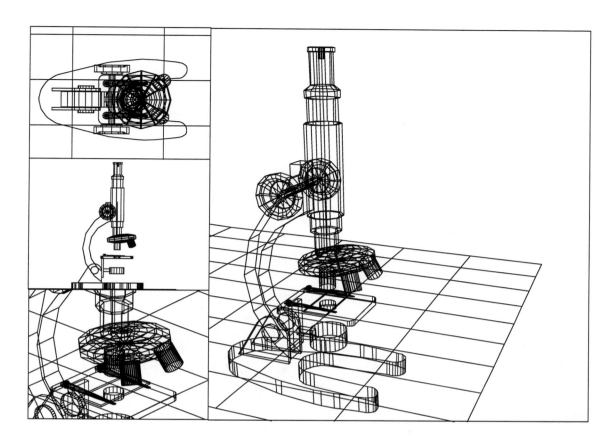

To see the effect of smooth shading

Close any open toolbars to save space on the screen. You need only the Render toolbar for this exercise. Begin by rendering the perspective view of the microscope in the large viewport using the default values for lights, materials, scenes, and color palette.

1   *From the View menu, choose Toolbars and then choose Render.*

AutoCAD 2005 displays the Render toolbar. Move it to a convenient place on the screen.

2   *Make sure that the large viewport is active (so that the crosshairs are visible).*

3   *From the Render toolbar, choose Render.*

Render looks like this:

4   *In the Render dialog box, choose Render.*

The picture will look like this:

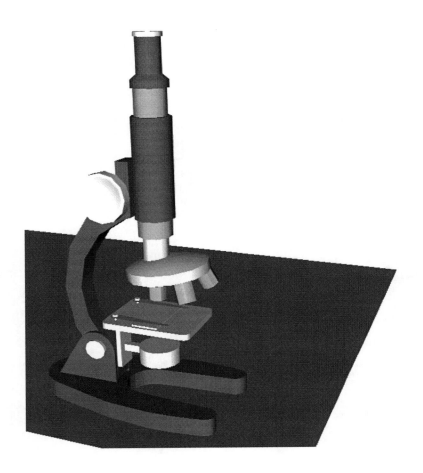

To save named views

You will save the viewpoints of the large viewport and the lower-left viewports as a named view. You will use the views later to create scenes, which are combinations of views and lights.

1   *On the command line, enter view*

     In The dialogbox choose New

     Make the *New View* **dialogbox look like this:**

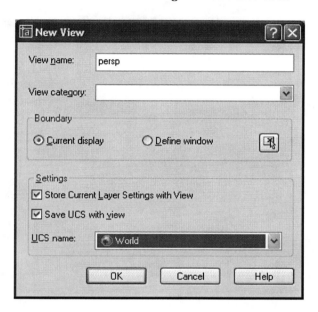

2   *Choose OK*

3   *Activate the lower-left viewport.*

4   *Save this view as* **closeup** *in the same way as* you saved **persp**

To add lights

In the following procedure, you will add two lights to the drawing: a distant light and a point light. Rays from a distant light are parallel like the light from the sun. Rays from a point light spread out from a central point, like the light from a light bulb.

1   *Activate the large viewport.*

2   *From the Render toolbar, choose Lights.*

     Lights looks like this:

3   *Set the ambient light intensity to 0.5.*

Ambient light is the overall level of illumination on all faces in the drawing. It has no specific source or direction.

4   *In the Lights dialog box, select Distant Light from the list and choose New.*

5   *In the New Distant Light dialog box, enter **sun** in the Light Name box and choose OK.*

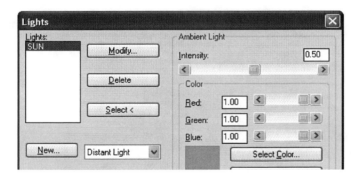

6   *Select Point Light from the list and choose New.*

7   *In the New Point Light dialog box, enter **lamp** in the Light Name box.*

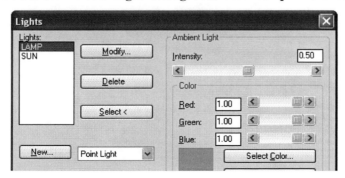

You can specify the exact location of the light.

8   *Choose Modify - you leave the dialogbox and you have to enter the coordinates on the command line*

Enter light location <current>: **6,6,6**

9   *Choose OK twice to exit the dialog boxes.*

Note: The third coordinate is for the Z axis.

To create scenes

In this procedure, you will add two scenes based on the lights and the views you created earlier.

1   *From the Render toolbar, choose Scenes.*

Scenes looks like this:

2   *In the Scenes dialog box, choose New.*

3   *In the New Scene dialog box, enter **SCENE1** in the Scene Name box.*

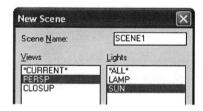

On the left is the list of views and on the right is the list of lights.

4   *Select **PERSP** for the view and **SUN** for the light.*

5   *Choose OK to exit the New Scene dialog box*

.

6   *Repeat steps 2 through 5 to create a second scene called **SCENE2** with a **CLOSEUP** view and a **LAMP** light.*

7   *Choose OK twice to exit the dialog boxes.*

To render using scenes

Try rendering, using the two scenes you have created.

1   *From the Render toolbar, choose Render.*

2   *In the Render dialog box, select Smooth Shade.*

3   *Select SCENE2 and choose Render*

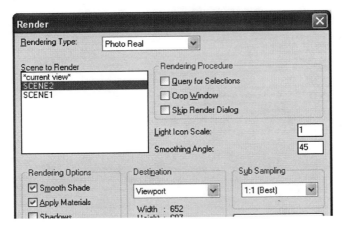

The rendered image should look like the one shown in the following illustration. The light is much brighter and the colors stronger than the earlier rendering. If the image seems too dark, try increasing the ambient-light intensity.

Your drawing should look like this.

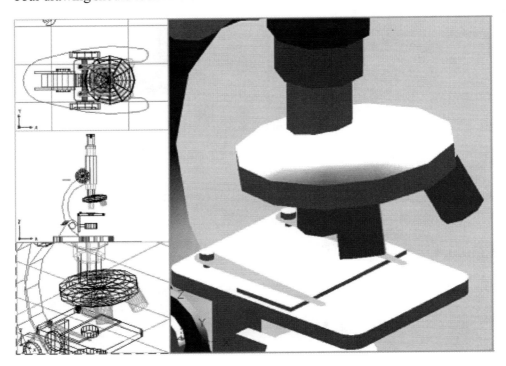

3   Render the image again using SCENE1.

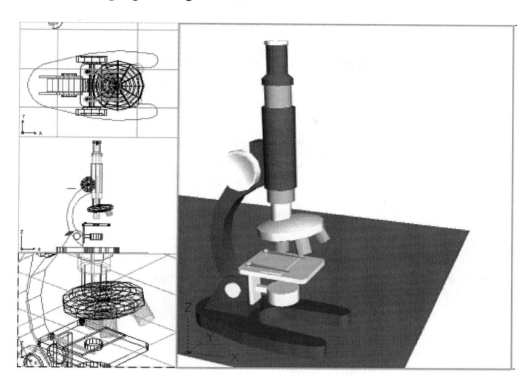

To create new materials

You can make your renderings more realistic by attaching materials to the objects that make up your model. For example, you can make a surface look like shiny metal or nonreflective wood. In the next two procedures, you will create some new materials and attach them to objects in the drawing that are a particular color.

1   *From the Render toolbar, choose Materials.*

   Materials looks like this:

2   *In the Materials dialog box, choose New.*

3   *In the New Standard Material dialog box, enter* **GOLD** *in the Material Name box.*

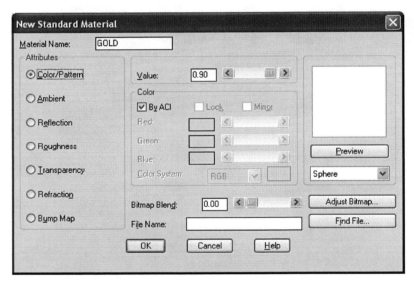

AutoCAD 2005 gives you complete control over the color and reflective qualities of the surface material.

4   *Under Attributes, choose Color/Pattern and set the value to 0.9.*

5   *Set the values for Ambien to 0.2*
     Reflection to 0.8
     Roughness 0.3

6   *Choose OK to exit New Standard Material dialog box.*

7   *Choose Preview to see the effect of all the settings.*

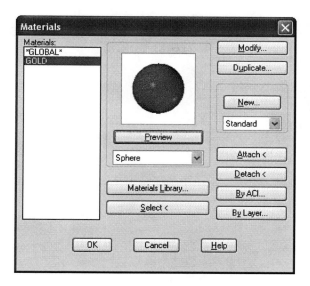

The sphere shows what the material will look like when it's attached to objects in the drawing. It gives the effect of dull metal.

8   *Choose OK.*

To attach materials to colors

Continue by attaching the material **GOLD** to a color in the drawing.

1   *In the Materials dialog box, choose By ACI*

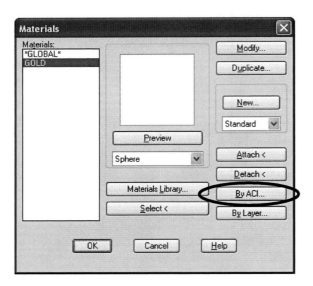

ACI stands for AutoCAD 2005 color index, which is the list of numbers assigned to the AutoCAD 2005 colors.

2   *In the Attach by AutoCAD 2005 Color Index dialog box, select 2 (Yellow) from the list and choose Attach.*

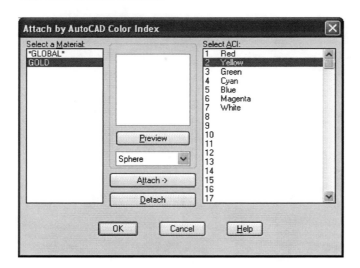

3   *Choose OK.*

4   *Create and attach the other materials, as follows:*

Material	**TUBE**
Color/Pattern	0.40
Ambient	0.30
Reflection	0.20
Roughness	0.10
Attach to	3 (green)

Material	**METAL**
Color/Pattern	0.70
Ambient	0.30
Reflection	1.00
Roughness	0.50
Attach to	7 (white)

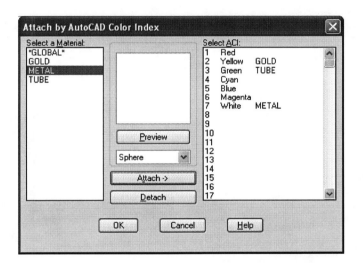

5   *Choose OK twice to exit the dialog boxes.*

To render the final image

To finish the exercise, render the model with the materials attached.

1   *From the Render toolbar, choose Render.*

2   *In the Render dialog box, choose More Options.*

3   *In the Render Options dialog box, select Phong for Render quality and then choose OK.*
Phong rendering gives the best quality for the final image.

4   *In the Render dialog box, select SCENE1 then choose Render.*

The rendered image should look like the one shown in the following illustration:

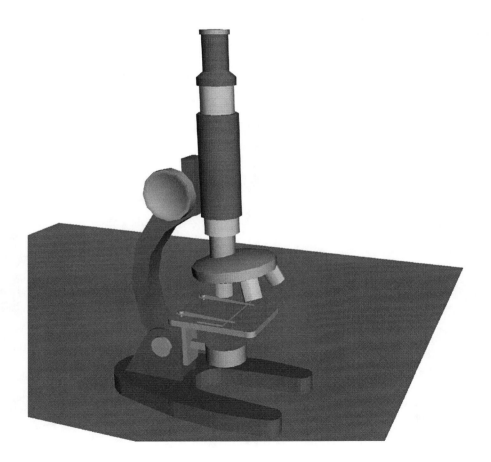

Tutorial 10 - Using Layout and Xrefs

When you draw in AutoCAD, you will usually work in model space. When you want to plot your drawing, you will switch to layout. This lesson introduces you to layout by showing you how to lay out a sheet of drawings for plotting. You don't have to use layout to plot a drawing, but with it you can place several views of a drawing at different scales in separate viewports. You can also control the visibility of the layers in those viewports.

The lesson consists of eight short procedures:

- Creating the drawing file
- Setting up the layout environment
- Creating and scale the first viewport
- Changing the viewport size and scale
- Opening two new viewports
- Externally referencing other drawings
- Scaling the viewports
- Adding a title block

To create the drawing file

The file **lesson10.dwt** is an AutoCAD 2005 template that contains some of the preliminary setup work for this exercise. To take advantage of this setup, you will create a new drawing file using **lesson10.dwt** as a template. When you are ready to create the file for this exercise, follow these steps:

1   *From the File menu, choose New.*
2   *In the Create New Drawing dialog box, choose Use a Template.*
3   *In the Select a Template box, select the file lesson10.dwt and choose OK.*

AutoCAD 2005 opens a new drawing file with the settings from the template you have specified. The drawing area contains the floor plan shown in the illustration.

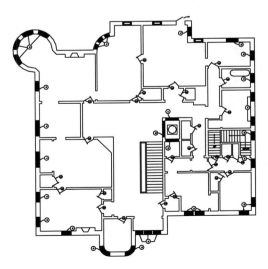

Layout

1   *Rightclick the* **LAYOUT1** *tab and choose* **Page Setup Manager...**

In the Page Setup Manager dialog box choose **Modify**

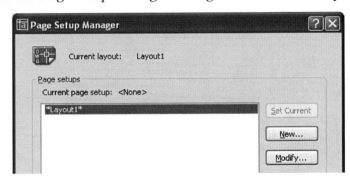

In the **Page Setup** *dialogbox choose*

DWF ePlot device.pc3 as plot device and the papersize
ARCH expand E1 (30.00x42.00 inches).

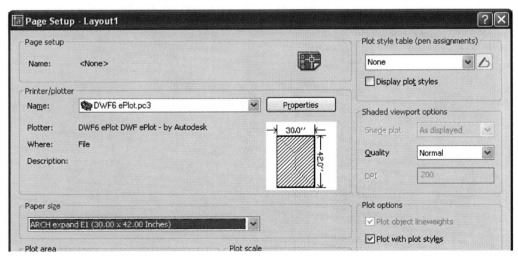

Click OK and Close

Scale the first viewport

1   *Click at the border of the viewport at move it to the layer called* **BORDER**

2   *Make the upper right grip active and move it to the upper right corner of the paper (inside the dashed line).*

3   *In the* **VIEW** *menu choose the toolbar* **VIEWPORTS**

4   *Make the viewport active by doubleclicking inside the border.*

5   *In the* **VIEWPORTS** *toolbar choose the scalefactor 1/4" = 1'*

6   **PAN the drawing to the left side of the viewport.**

7   *Doubleclick outside the border to make the paper active and drag the border simular to the drawing. In the right side of the viewport there are place for 2 new viewports.*

8   *Choose the* **Single Viewport** *from the viewports toolbar to draw 2 new viewports on the paper*

The layout should now look like this:

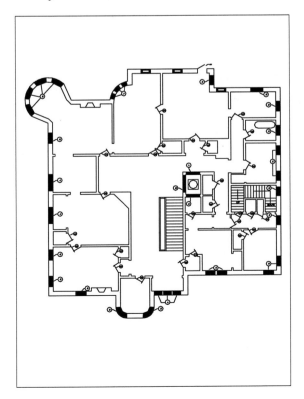
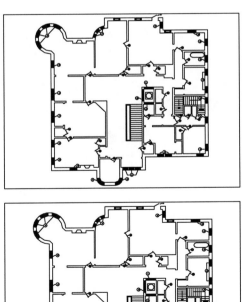

We don´t want to see the same drawing in all 3 viewport. In the two new viewports we will freeze the layers so the viewports look empty.

9   *Make the upper-right viewport active and freeze all the layers starting with Z*

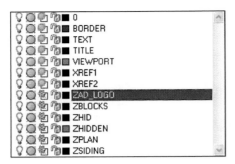

When you click the layer drop down, the viewport looks empty.

Do the same in the lower-right viewport.

To externally reference other drawings

Now you can place a second drawing in one of the new viewports using an xref.

About Xrefs

In AutoCAD, you use the XREF command to insert other drawings in the current drawing. By keeping drawings as external files and cross-referencing them with this method, you will ensure that any changes that you make to the cross-referenced file are reflected automatically in the current drawing. Unlike blocks, cross-referenced files do not become part of the drawing's database.

1   *Make XREF1 the current layer.*

Make sure the upper-right viewport is active. Activate the upper-right viewport by picking inside.

2   *On the command line, enter* **XREF**

Choose **Attach** *in the dialogbox and find the drawing* **ELEV1.DWG** *where you have placed it.*

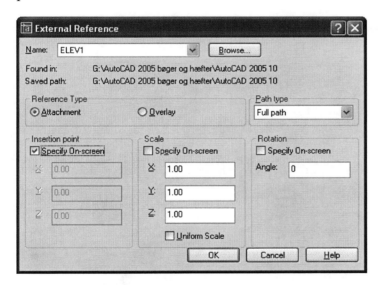

Choose OK and place the drawing in the lower left corner of the viewport.

The new drawing is inserted in all three viewports. To suppress the display of the xref, you will freeze the XREF1 layer in the other viewports.

3   *Select the large viewport on the left.*

4   *From the Layer drop down list choose Freeze in current viewport for the layer XREF1*

Freeze/Thaw in current viewport looks like this:

The xref drawing is no longer visible in the viewport.

5   *Repeat step 4 to freeze the xref drawing from the third viewport after making that viewport current.*

6   *Make XREF2 the current layer, then repeat steps 2 through 4 to xref* **ELEV2.DWG** *into the third viewport and clear it from the other viewports.*

Your drawing should look like this.

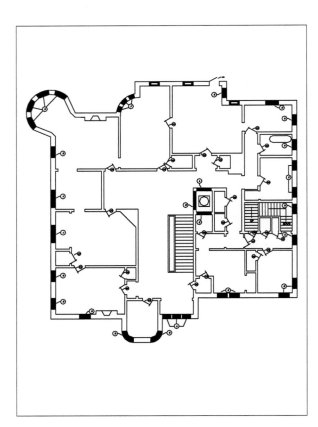

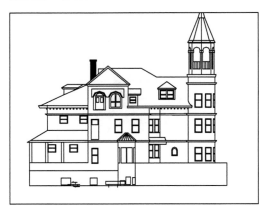

Index

Symboler

-xref 91

A

About Absolute Coordinates 8
About Hatch Scale 29
About Layers 14
About Object Selection 11
About Perpendicular Object Snap and Ortho Mode
    23
About Polar Coordinates 31
About Relative Coordinates 16
About Selecting with an object snap 10
About Text Height 46
About the CHAMFER Command 34
About the CIRCLE Command 7
About the Continue Option 39
About the OFFSET Command 8
About the TRIM Command 13
About the VPOINT Command 36
About the ZOOM Command 7
About Xrefs 91
Absolute Coordinates 8
Arc 18, 52
Array 60
ATTDISP 67
Attributes 61
AutoCAD Template 6

B

Baseline Dimension 40
block 57

C

CHAMFER 34
CHAMFER Command 34
CIRCLE 6, 7
CIRCLE Command 7
Continue Option 39
Continued Dimension 39

D

ddatte 70
dimension 38
Drawing a Flange 6
Drawing Aids 7
Drawing aids 6
drawing environment 6
Drawing Limits 7

Drawing units 6

E

Entering Commands 5
Erase 68
ESC 5
EXTEND 25

F

FILLET 21, 33

H

HATCH 21, 29
Hatch Scale 29
HIDE 36

I

INSERT 59

L

Layer 14
Layers 6, 14
LEADER 47
lesson01.dwt 6
lesson02.dwt 14
lesson03.dwt 21
lesson04.dwt 31
lesson05.dwt 37
lesson06.dwt 45
lesson07.dwt 50
lesson08.dwt 61
lesson09.dwt 74
lesson10.dwt 87
Lights 78
Limits 6
LINE 6
Line 10
Linear Dimension 38
Linetypes 6

M

materials 82
MIRROR 6, 11
MLEDIT 20
Move 69
Multiline 16
Multiline Text 46

N

named views 77
New 14

O

Object Selection 11
object snap 10
OFFSET 6, 9, 23
Offset 8
OFFSET Command 8
Overview 4

P

Paper size 6
Paper Space 87
Perpendicular Object Snap and Ortho Mode 23
Polar Coordinates 31
Polygon 54
Polyline 32
Preface 2

R

Radius Dimension 44
Rectangle 62
Relative Coordinates 16
RENDER 74
Revolve 35
revolve 35
Rotate 69

S

Scenes 79
Smooth Shade 80
Snap to Center 11
Snap to Intersection 69
Snap to Midpoint 22, 57
Snap to Perpendicular 23
Snap to Tangent 10
solid 35
Speed Tip 9

T

Template 2
Text Height 46
Text Style 46
Thaw 92
Tips 5
To add a table and define attributes for it 62
To add lights 77
To calculate the area of the cubicle 71
To change layers for the offset lines 24
To change the viewpoint and hide lines 35
To create a doorway 20
To create a new layer 14
To create a new text style 46
To create a revolved solid model 35

To create paragraph text 46
To create scenes 79
To create the drawing file
    6, 14, 21, 31, 37, 45, 50, 61, 74, 87
To dimension a radius 44
To dimension the front 41
To dimension the top edge 40
To draw a chair 54
To draw a line to connect the bottoms of the two b
    10
To draw leaders with attached notes 47
To draw the bottom part of the bushing assembly
    21
To draw the door and swing 17
To draw the kitchen doors 51
To draw the profile of the hub 31
To draw the room walls 17
To draw the table and insert the chairs 59
To draw two bushings 7
To edit the attributes 70
To erase objects from the office layout 67
To extend the center lines of both holes 25
To finish drawing the bushing assembly outline 27
To hatch the completed outline 29
To make the chair into a block 57
To make the table into a block 65
To make the table into a block and insert it in th 65
To mirror the line to connect the tops of the bush
    10
To move the computer 69
To render using scenes 80
To save named views 75
To see the effect of smooth shading 75
To set up the drawing environment 6
To trim the unwanted portion of the flange 13
TRIM 6, 13
TRIM Command 13
Tutorial 1 11
Tutorial 1 - Drawing a Flange 11
Tutorial 10 87
Tutorial 10 - Using Paper Space and Xrefs 87
Tutorial 2 14
Tutorial 2 - Drawing a Room 14
Tutorial 3 26
Tutorial 3 - Drawing a Bushing Assembly 26
Tutorial 4 31
Tutorial 4 - Drawing a Hub 31
Tutorial 5 37
Tutorial 5 - Dimensioning Your Drawing 37
Tutorial 6 45
Tutorial 6 - Using Text 45
Tutorial 7 50
Tutorial 7 - Drawing a Kitchen Floor Plan 50

Tutorial 8 61
Tutorial 8 - Using Attributes 61
Tutorial 9 74
Tutorial 9 - Rendering Your Drawing 74

U

Using the AutoCAD Tutorial 5

V

viewport 89
VPOINT 36
VPOINT Command 36

W

Welcome to the AutoCAD Tutorial 5

X

XREF 91
Xrefs 87, 91

Z

ZOOM All 7
ZOOM Command 7
Zoom Previous 56
Zoom Window 55